VFX EXPLAINED

TECHNOLOGIES HOLLYWOOD USE TO MAKE FILMS !

ABHISHEK KANGE

I dedicate this book to my Parents

Contents

I

INTRODUCTION TO VFX

Many of us don't know what vfx really is ? How are Vfx made ? Can you add vfx to your mobile shot video? What technology and Instruments are used ? and more such questions will be answered as you start to read this book ahead.

Before understanding what vfx is , let's understand what is video editing . Video Editing as simple as it sounds is to edit a video. In video editing we perform some most basic operations such as cutting the video at certain points and removing the parts of video we don't want , we add transitions etc. There is a lot and a lot more in editing but the basic aim of video editing is to make the final video so that we have all shots properly aligned in a sequence according to our story . Again the editing of sound and adding sound effects at particular places too comes under video editing .

જી

Now comes What is VFX? In VFX we manipulate the contents of the shot . As in video editing we just organised the video and didn't manipulate any contents of the shot which is done in VFX .

We use the VFX to manipulate the scene as we want. Today we can create anything you can imagine using vfx tools and knowledge (if you have proper knowledge and practice).

Before going further and exploring the beautiful world of VFX , let's first see the History of VFX.

HISTORY OF VFX

Do you know that even before the digital era when movies were shot on photographic films, VFX existed. Yes it had limitations . Today most of the vfx work is done after the video is shot (in post production) but before the digital era , people used to do vfx during shooting the video . They would follow some techniques to fake the scenes. E.g If you want to show a huge set which is not possible to build then they used to make paintings and would align them with the shot such that it looked like it was the real place. Today all this is replaced by VFX that is done in post production using computers.

Process of VFX Creation :

Now further we will start discussing how VFX is created . What are the techniques used to create such vfx? What all softwares is used ? Who all people are involved and many such interesting things will be discussed.

VFX as it sounds is not a very simple process but a combination of different processes which are carried out by different people. Suppose you want to create a scene of a dinosaur attacking a person , then there are many departments involved to create this one shot . Firstly you have to create the 3D- dinosaur (Called as CGI - computer generated imaginary) in dedicated softwares. This is done by the Modelling Department which takes care of all such processes. Then you have to color it to give it the look of a dinosaur, you have to make it's skin as it originally looks, its eyes and other things.This is called Texturing , This is done by another department which is dedicated to study and create textures. Now the Dinosaur's model is ready but it's not moving , not performing any actions. You have to Animate it so that it can move ahead, Open its mouth and attack the person. All animations are taken care of by another department which is dedicated to animation only. Now we come to video footage , before placing the dinosaur you have to analyze the movements of the camera, how the camera has moved and then using this you place the dinosaur in your footage . This process is called MatchMoving.

Then we have the composting , where everything is brought together and final output is created. This was a small example but there are many other things which will be discussed further in upcoming chapters.

II

CHAPTER : 3D MODELLING

Modelling as it spells is to mold something to create some interesting things. You may probably know how pottery is made . We use clay to create pottery of any shape and size and whatever look we want. Similarly the software provides us with a Mesh (clay) as and the VFX Artist used it to create what they want by using the tools present in the softwares.

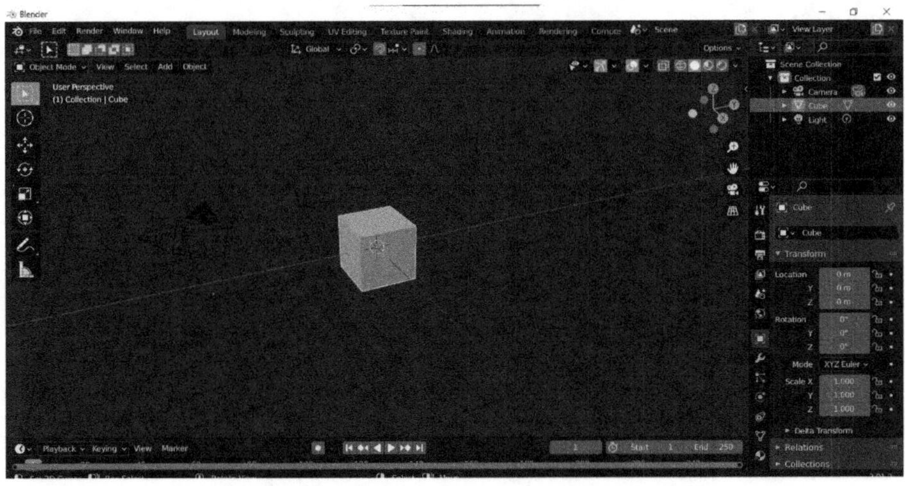

Picture1.1 : cube made up of mesh in a 3d software. This can be further molded into different objects .

ଞ

What are 3D Softwares ?

All these computer generated models are created in a three dimensional space . The softwares used for designing such 3D models provide you a 3 dimensional environment where you can create your models.

Such software are also called 3D softwares in day to day language.These 3D software does not limit them to creating 3d models. You can add materials to your models i.e add textures , you can animate the models. These 3d softwares plays a major role in creating 3-D

environments for green screen replacement which we will discuss further in detail.You probably would have seen an animated movie like Toy Story and Cars 2 etc. These movies are created in such 3D softwares too. The environment such as buildings , roads , interior , mountains, valley and so on are created in these software . And then the 3D models are animated and placed in the 3D environment and then they are rendered out (get final video output).These softwares also play a very major role in creating FX . Now what is fx .This we are going to see in detail in further but for short , you would have seen the effects like destruction, SciFi effects, ground collapse , lightning effects in many movies. These are all FX . These are also created in such 3D softwares and then integrated into your footage.This is still not the end of your 3d software.

Picture1.2 Toy Story , animated movie. Image source : wikipedia

Another big place where Modelling plays an important role is the gaming industry.

You might have played games like NFS , and much more real world games. All the assets used in games like the cars, trees, road tracks , characters of game etc are first created in such 3D softwares and later they are used in games. So modelling also has a very important role in the gaming industry.

Sculpting :

Another important part of 3D modelling is , sculpting. Before understanding sculpting ,you must first understand how modelling is done. Modelling is based on polygon . In modelling , 3D models are made by manipulating polygons. It's not like molding clay and creating something. Here you have primitive shapes and you adjust, add , manipulate it's faces , vertices , edges etc to create different shapes.

But sculpting is something different. Here we don't directly work with polygons. Here we have a mesh like clay and then we are free to mold it into any shape as we want. We can make more organic models like human faces,and models where we want high end details.

Whereas modelling is used for making hard objects like buildings , cars , etc which can be created by manipulating different polygons.

Picture1.3 : Depicts a sculpted 3D Model.
imageSource:www.AnimationWorlds.com

Texturing the 3D models :

Say you modelled a character or say a Dinosaur. But actually it doesn't not look like dinosaur, it's all white (basic Color of any 3D object). So now you have to study the colour of body of dinosaur, it's eyes, its tail , it's hair , it's nails ,it's foot, and all the details. After studying these textures you have to create those textures. Textures are created as a image format and later projected onto the 3D model.

Not so easy , it's not only the image that you have to project onto the dinosaur but you also have to consider the bumps and depths , the roughness of skin, the reflections of skin , you have to make all these textures too and apply inorder to achieve realistic results.

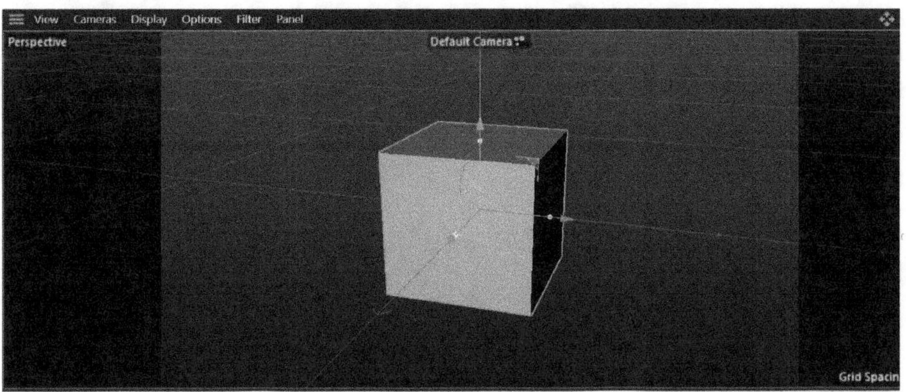

Picture1.4 : 3D cube with no texture

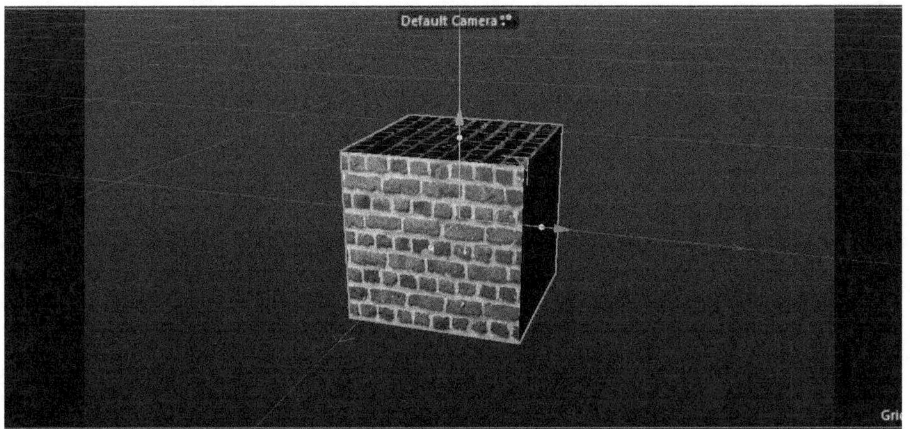

Picture1.5: 3D cube with an image texture , the image texture makes the cube look like a brick.

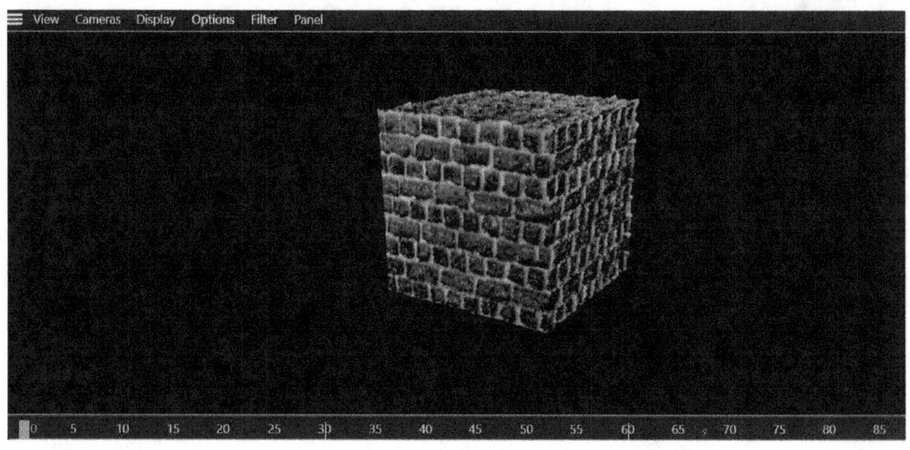

Picture1.6: 3D cube with bump texture.

Elements of 3D modelling softwares :

These elements of 3D modelling which we will discuss now are a very important part inorder to understand the 3D concept

1.Camera :

In 3D software you can create a virtual camera. You might think what is need of a camera in 3D software.

3D softwares provide you a 3 dimensional view , that is you can view your scenes from any angle you want. You can move anywhere in the 3D environment.But at the time of creating a final video out of your scene(if you are creating an animated movie) .Then you need to frame each scene from a certain angle and take out the output as a video. So you need a camera. Also the camera you create provides you with a lot of features of actual camera. You can adjust the focal length , this way you can create depth in your video , it provides all the features that a normal real camera provides you.

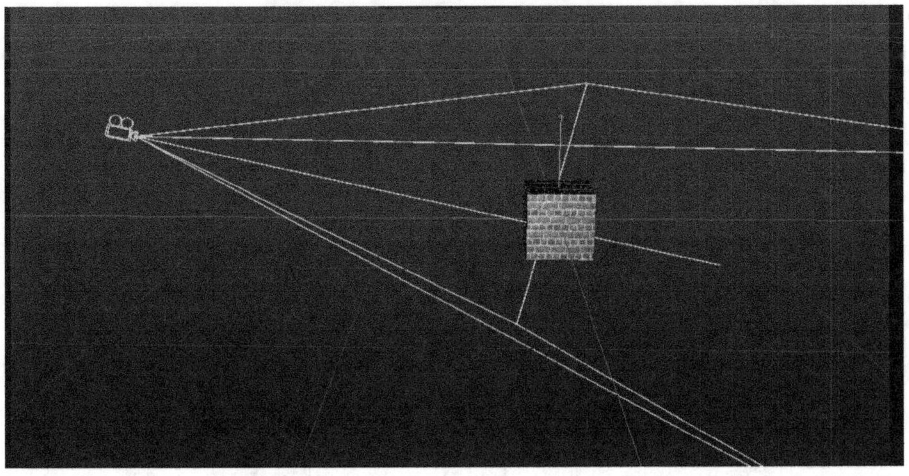

Picture1.7: Camera point the cube in a 3D space.

2.Lights

Your scene must be properly lighted inorder to get a good result. The 3D softwares also provide you with different types of lights . You can resize these lights, Move them anywhere in 3D space.

These lights acts same as the light in real life. They create shadows, reflection ,and works according to the material you applying to an object in scene. If you apply a metallic texture to your object then the light will bounce off the surface in a regular manner and you will be able to see reflection on the material. This is how important lights are in creating a 3D scene.

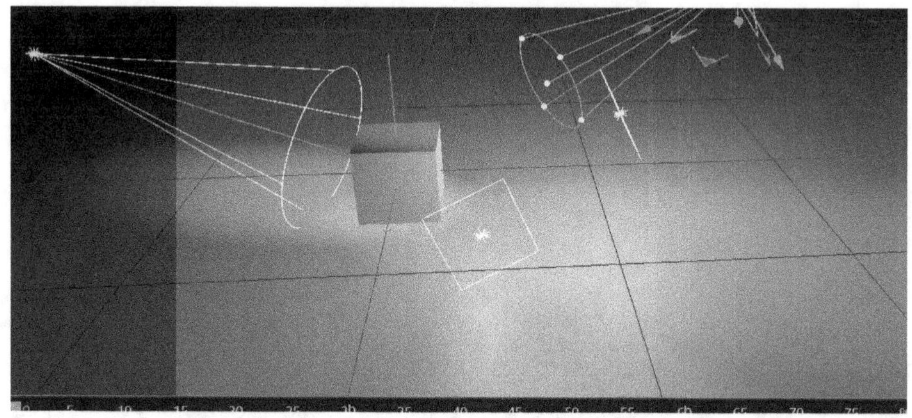

Different types of virtual lights used to illuminate the scene .

Popular Softwares for 3D Modelling :
   1.Autodesk Maya

This is a very very popular Software for most of the 3D Works.
This software has become the industry standard. Almost all VFX studios use this softwares for most of their 3D World.
   2.Autodesk 3dsMax

This is also a great 3d software designed by the same company. But this is more used in architecture purposes to design 3d models of buildings etc. But yes it is used sometimes as per requirement.
   3.Blender
   This is an open source free 3d software which everyone can use. This software is also great for beginners. I too started with this software because it provides you a very great start and clear your basics. This software is not used in the VFX industry for commercial purposes because it's free.
   4.Houdini
   This is the future of VFX. Houdini is not used for modelling but used for creating complex FX and it's a very very powerful software to create high end complex FX.
   5. Cinema 4D

This is also a great software for beginners. It has a very clean UI which makes it user friendly.This is also a great option if you have a small budget system.

• 11 •

III
ANIMATION

In the animation part , the 3D Characters created in modelling are animated.The 3d models are not directly animated.They are first Rigged.
   What is Rig ?

Let's say you have a human character and you have to make it walk. Then first you have to create a skeleton for the 3D model. You have to create a basic skeleton which has hands, neck, legs , fingers , etc. Then you have to link the skeleton with the 3D model. You have to properly attached the hand of the skeleton to the hand of the 3D model and similarly all parts.This process is called
Rigging.

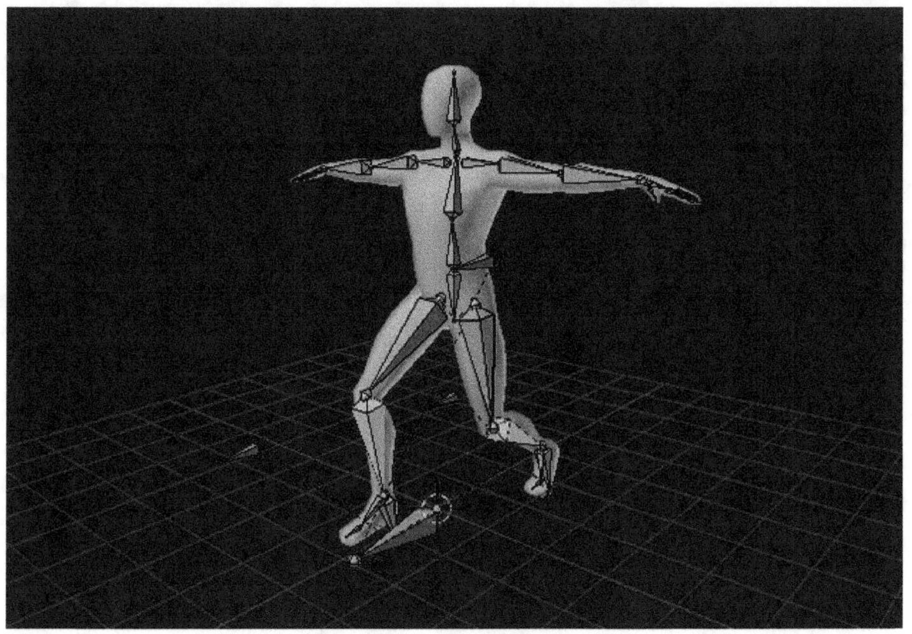

Picture of a rigged 3D character

Now comes the Animation part. We want our character to walk , the we will now just animate the skeleton legs and hence the legs will move , because skeleton is linked to the legs of 3D Character.

How is animation done ?

The most common animation that is used is the keyframe animation.So first you must understand what are keyframes and how they work. Let's understand this by an example of small 2D animation of a text. Say you have a text and you want to move the text from left to right on the screen . Then you position the text on left on the starting of the video and add a keyframe(i.e mark the position and note down the position using x,y coordinates).

Then you move to the end of your video and move the text to the other end and then add a keyframe. This way you note down the position of text in x,y coordinate at the last frame of the video.

Then the software automatically calculates the position of the text in the middle of the video such that the first keyframe is starting and the final position is the next keyframe. And your text moves from one keyframe (position) to another position. Such keyframes are not limited to only position but also to size and other attributes of objects.

Now let's see the working of keyframe animation in creating walking animation of the 3D characters. When you want to make your character walk then first you have to make his/her leg lift up and then move it front and then keep it back. So here we have 3 different motions whose compound movement gives us the walking animation of one step of the character. So here we have to use 3 keyframes. One for lifting the leg , another for moving the leg forward and another for keeping the foot down.

To make this keyframe you are given a Timeline (a line with time on it) and then you place the keyframe according to the time at which you want the motion to happen.

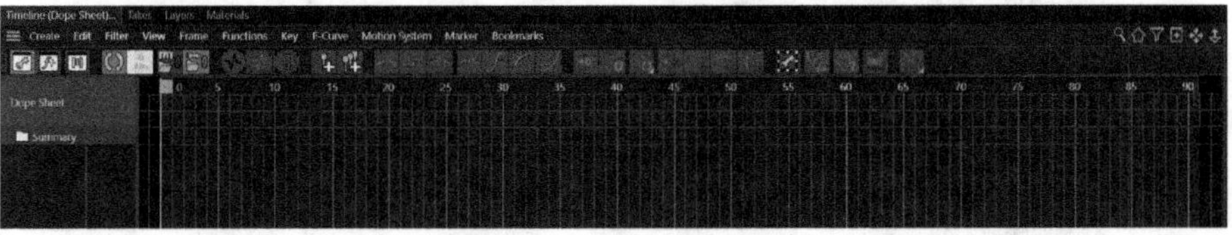

Now if you add a keyframe after 5 sec and at that point lift up the foot , In next 2sec add a keyframe and move the leg forward and in next 2sec place the leg down. Now the animation for one step and one leg is completed. Apply similar to another leg and for complete moving of character apply this same process for further steps. This way the walking animation is completed using keyframes. This keyframe animation is used to create complex animation too. It has a wide application .

But still keyframe animation does not help to achieve realistic and smooth results and also it's a very time consuming process.

With advancement in technology,a new technique is used to animate character. This is called Motion capture. This helps us to achieve the most realistic movement in our animation.

Motion Capturing :

In motion capture technique the motion/ movements of a real human actor are recorded and then these movements are projected on the Computer generated characters.

To do motion capture, the actors wore a special suit called motion capture suit and were supposed to act . The actions , facial motion are captured by camera and then the motion like if they are walking or talking are as it is imposed on the 3D character.

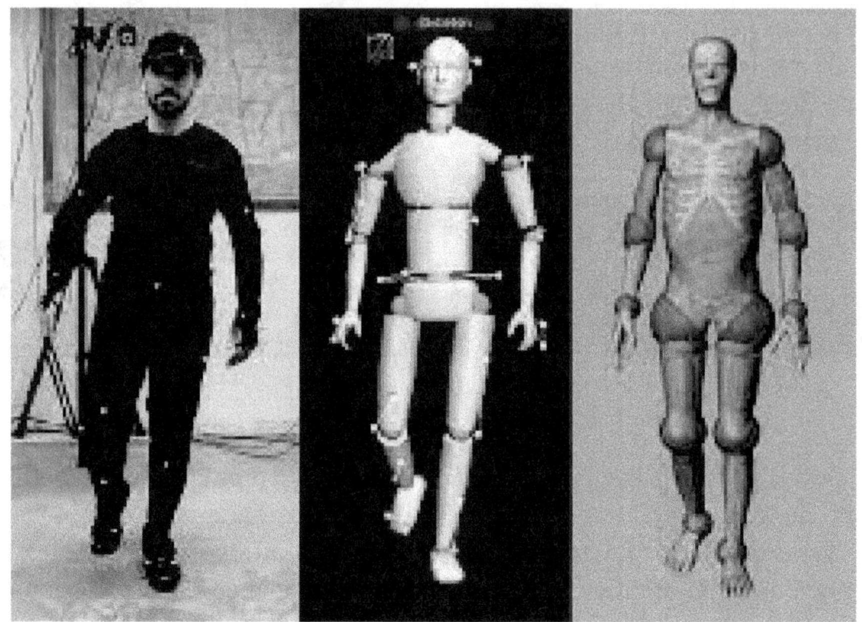

Motion capture

You have understood very well about rigs used to animate characters , rigs are the skeleton of 3d characters. Eg tiger, he has legs , head,body , so you have to have a skeleton to move them. But still you will find that your animation will not look real even if you have the perfect movement.

Because let's take the example of a tiger. When the tiger walks you have to also focus on other processes that take place like respiration which will continually take place. So you have to make the oscillatory motion of the chest. Hence you have to make muscles. Yes, in 3D software you also have an option to build muscle. So if you are animating something you first have to study it's each movement . How the motion of that thing or person takes place in real life. And then only your animation will look realistic.

Physics in Animation :

Have you ever heard that physics is important in animation? You wouldn't have heard it . Let's understand the importance of physics in Animation using an example.

Let's say you want to animate a ball falling from a certain height and bouncing back to a certain height.To do so you have to add physics to the ball. You have to tell the 3D software that this Ball is made of so and so material , it's weight is so and so and also make the surface of a material which allows bounciness.

Lets slowly understand this. You want the ball to bounce back but you told the software that it's metal ball and in other case you told that it's a rubber ball. In which case you think that the chances of bouncing back are more.Of Course in the second case. This way physics plays an important role.

Let's say you are animating a collision . If you made the physics of colloidal particle that of glass then the colloidal particle will break but if you made its properties of a metal then it will react differently. So as an animator you would also have knowledge of physics , How things work in real life .

IV

MATCHMOVING

Matchmoving as it sounds you might think that it may be related something to motion. You probably may be guessing something related to matching motion. Yes you are correct . To understand match moving you must first know how layer based video editing works.

Suppose you have shot a video when you went out for a trip and then you have to place a text on top of the video then you take another layer and add text on that . Now your video is in the background and the text is in the foreground . This is how layer based editing works.

Now you have shot a video in which you are moving from one end to another end and you want your text to stick to you.You want that if you added the text on your shirt it must stick to your shirt even if you go anywhere in the video.This won't happen on its own because the top layer of text is fixed, it does not have any motion. To make it stick to your shirt you have to add motion to it.

Now there are two ways to do it . You can manually give it motion by changing its position in each frame. This is a very very tough process. Because even if your video is of 10sec it contains 1000s of frames .So here comes the magic of matchmoving.

This process of matching your layer with existing footage is called matchmoving.

Matchmoving is a broader term , it has many different processes.We will now discuss all those processes one by one and try to understand why they are important in creating VFX.

Important note is that Matchmoving plays a very important role in creating VFX , it's very important to have this process very very accurate inorder to make your VFX look realistic or all your hard work will go in vain. Hence a separate department is assigned which is focused on only doing matchmoving.

৪৩

1. 2- D Tracking :

Let's again understand 2-D Tracking using an example. You have a video in which a person is moving and you have to call out on the person. If you don't know what a call out is , see the below image.

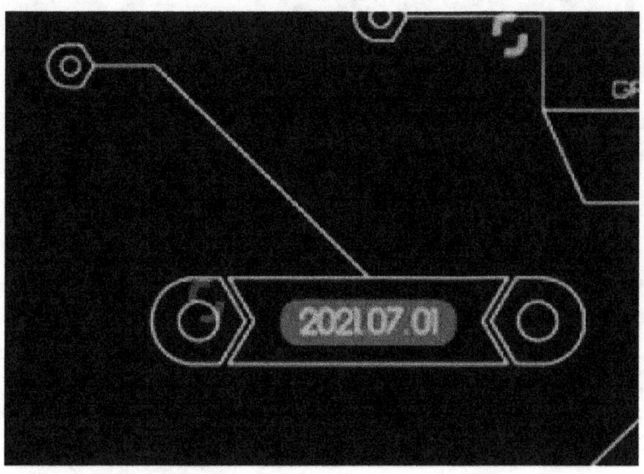

picture : Call Out

Now first you have to track how the person is moving in the video. The software provides you with a tracking marker which you place on the point which you want to track. In this case you can use the person's head. This tracker locates the point to which it is attached in each frame. Then this data is used by the software to analyse the motion of the head . Now we have the data and we can add this data to our call out and it will now remain fixed to our person.

*The call out now sticks to person's head where
so ever he moves in frame*

This example was very simple to just understand the basis of 2 -D tracking but it is very important in many different cases , like replacing sky , replacing green and blue screen etc. which we will discuss further in the book.

Softwares used for 2-D Tracking :

2-D Tracking is not done in the softwares which are dedicated for matchmoving.This is because 2-D is mainly used during Compositing , so all compositing software contains the feature of 2 -D Tracking.

3D Camera Tracking :

Yes you guessed it right this type of tracking is used for tracking 3D environments. Let's understand in a simple way with an example. Remember we have discussed 3D Modelling . Now we are going to use that 3D models and add them to our video using 3D Camera Tracking.

3D camera Tracking is used when your camera, if not fixed , it's moving and shooting in all directions.It's also important if you want to add 3D Models in your video. During this process of Camera Tracking , the software understands how the camera has moved . Using this information it creates a 3D environment . This data is then linked to the 3D model .Now your model is placed in the video at the correct position even if your scene moves here and there.

Object Tracking :

Object Tracking , this is one of my favourite topics. Have you seen movies in which actors pick up animals in their hand or fight with a tiger or fly on a dragon? Yes the animals , the dragon are 3D
modelled characters,but have you ever thought how they do this. Here object Tracking plays a very important role.

Let's understand this with a simple example. We have to design a shot where we have to pick an animal in our hand. At the time of shooting we use a prop with some tracking markers, see the picture below.

picture source : Image from game of thrones behind the scenes.

Using the Object Tracking we track this prop object. The software understands how the object is moving in 3d spaces, using this we generate tracking data and then apply this data to the object with which we have to replace the prop. Now your 3D character will follow the same movement as the prop are doing.This is the way object tracking works.

Another best example , if you have seen the movie Bahubali returns then you will notice that when Bahubali's mother took the child and in flowing water she held the boy up out of water in her hand. During shooting it was a prop, which was replaced with a 3D Modelled boy using the same concept of Object Tracking.

picture source : bahubali 2 vfx breakdown

Softwares used for Matchmoving :
1. PFTrack
2. 3d Equalizer
3. Syntheyes

3d Equalizer is mostly used in most VFX Studios.

V
ROTOSCOPY

By just reading the title of this chapter you cannot guess what is Rotoscopy. Before you understand what is Rotoscopy, you must know why green and blue screens are

Green screens or Blue screen are used to replace the background. Let's understand how it works to better understand why green/blue screens are used.

Chroma keying : This is a technique using which we can choose a colour and then convert all the pixels of that color into transparent pixels..

So if we use a green screen behind our character and then use green chroma keying then all green pixels will be converted to transplant pixels and we have only our character and our required things on the screen. Now if we place another image behind this video then we have a new background behind our subject. See the below picture to understand better.

Why only green / Blue screens are used ?

This is because green is a distinct colour. It is not commonly used . We cannot use an orange or yellow screen because similar colour pixels are of our skin colour and they also get semi transparent. So green being a distinct colour is used. If we have a green colour in our subject , in that case we use a blue screen.

This way using green and blue screen we can separate the subject from background in order to change the background .

Green screen is not only used for removing background but also for replacement which we will discuss in further chapters. This much information is enough for you to understand
Rotoscopy.

There are many cases when we cannot use a green screen to separate the subject from the background , so we cut out the subject (called as mask out or roto out) frame by frame. We cut the subject in each frame. This process is called Rotoscopy.

Rotoscopy is not Limited to only replacing the background but it has a wide range of applications and hence plays a very major role in the process of VFX.See the below image to understand what is Rotoscopy in a better way

1. Rotoscopy for background replacement:

As discussed above we mask out or roto out the subject from its background and then place it onto another background that we want.
2. Rotoscopy for background and foreground separation :

This may be tricky so let's understand this by two examples, one very simple and another better example.Let's say you have a person in your video and you have to place a text behind your subject (the person in the video). To do so you first separate the subject from the background using Rotoscopy and then you place your text between your subject and background .

The above example was a very simple one , but now let's say you want to composite a car accident and explosion behind the subject then also you have to roto out the subject and then place the fx behind the subject.

3. Rotoscopy for Prep Out (Object Removal) :

tIn many cases your video has some unwanted object , they might be stationary or moving , eg people. So you have to remove them from your video. You have to do this also by using Rotoscopy. You have to remove them from each frame.

Softwares used for Rotoscopy :

1. Silhoutte FX - This is a software which is specially designed for Rotoscopy. It provides you with lot of tools to make the process of Rotoscopy more efficient.

2.Rotoscopy at small scale can be done in compositing softwares itself. E.g After effects , Nuke , fusion etc.

VI

FX

Welcome to FX. This is the place where all of the magic takes place.

You see the destruction that takes place in movies like ground collapse, building falling , bridge breaking down , all this is done by this department.

How do they make that building collapse ?

Have you ever wondered how they make that building collapse in the movie? As you have understood the previous chapters, now you can easily understand this. Let's say you want to make a. Building to collapse beside a road. You will first shoot a video of that road . Then you will matchmove that video so that you have all the camera motion and the 3d view of your place . Then you send all this data to the 3D software .

Now you have the virtual camera in 3d software and then in front of that camera you create a 3D building. Then you divide the building into several parts (cut the building into random parts). Then you add physics to the building , which we have discussed in the Animation part. Due to physics now the building will get destroyed into several parts and fall apart. But still it will not look like a building collapsing. Because when buildings collapse there is lots of dust. So in the same 3d software you can create smoke which we will discuss further . Then you also add the smoke into it and now your destruction of the building is ready in 3d World , now it's sent to the compositor who adds it to a video of whom we will talk about in further chapters.

Such buildings are created and later destructed in the software and then added to footage

Let's see what all FX artists make.Have you seen large waterfalls ? These are made by them. Ok but what's cool about that.They create the waterfall, that is they create the water simulation. They create the flow of water . While creating the simulation they have to focus on different things , it's not like an Instagram filter. They have to decide the flow , the direction, and the Physics. They first have to study the original waterfall . How they flow , at what height they look like. Because if you look at waterfalls , at large heights they behave differently and when they come down to lower height they behave differently.

How are these water simulations created in 3D software?

The 3D software provides you with a basic water simulation with different properties of that simulation. You have to adjust these properties and create the desired simulation.

Smoke Simulation

These are one of the most important simulations that are carried out nowadays.You would have seen the Thanos portail.This is an example of smoke simulation. This simulation is used most of the time. There are lots and lots of places where it is used and now it's become common. For example in the Aladdin's lamp when the genie comes out of there is special type of smoke , when jets fly in movies which are cgi planes you need the smoke , in destruction you need smoke, if you have fire in scene you need to simulate another type of smoke, if you have horror scenes then you need smoke. Very good example of smoke simulation is used in Harry Potter movies where you will find a lot of smoke simulation . This all is done by the FX department.

Fire simulation :

You get to different types of fires. You have explosions ,you have volcanoes, etc. All this is simulated in the 3d software itself and then composited onto the video at proper place using matchmove data.

Crowd simulation :

Have you seen lots of armies in war? They are not real. Yes, few people who are visible are real but all others are cgi models. These are also simulated by fx artists. 3d characters are created and animated and then they are multiplied and a random motion is added to them and you get that look that you have a massive crowd.

Another way of doing this is by recording a few people on a green screen and then multiplying them.

VII
COMPOSITING

According to me this is the best part of all the processes involved in VFX. This is because all of the final output is made here. The modelling department creates the 3D models , Texturing artists create the texture. Rigging department creates the rig , the animation department creates the animation , the FX department creates the FX , at last all this comes to the compositor and he creates the final composite. There are a lot of interesting processes involved in composting. We will discuss them now in some detail. Let's first understand what a compositor actually does. Take a look a below image , you have a green screen footage, a cgi model, a fx fire. And see the final output . The compositor integrates all the elements in its proper place using compositing software.

Green / Blue Screen replacement :

This is the most basic task you here about when you get your eyes to compositing.

As we discussed , the blue and green screen are used to replace the background in most cases.

Tracking markers on green / Blue Screen -

See the image, you would have seen such markers many times and you may have thought why these markers are used.

These markers are used to track the position of the subject, it's scale, rotation etc.so that it could be tracked and the subject may be linked to background.

Camera Projection :

This is a very important technique which is used nowadays . Before the advent of VFX , if you want to shoot at a required location, suppose a castle, then you have to create the set of the castle.If you want to show a person walking through the gate of the castle you have to create the castle set and road set.

But nowadays,with technology this can be achieved without creating such large sets which requires large financial investment.

Today all these things can be projected over 3D sets on the computer. See the below image where a 3D set is created using camera projection.

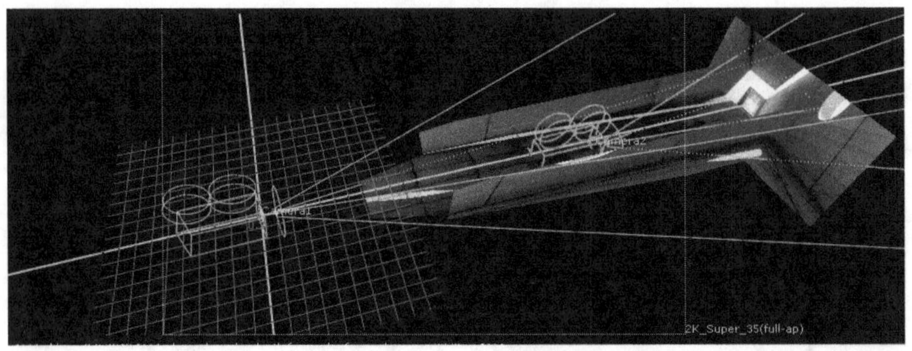

3 D set created in compositing software

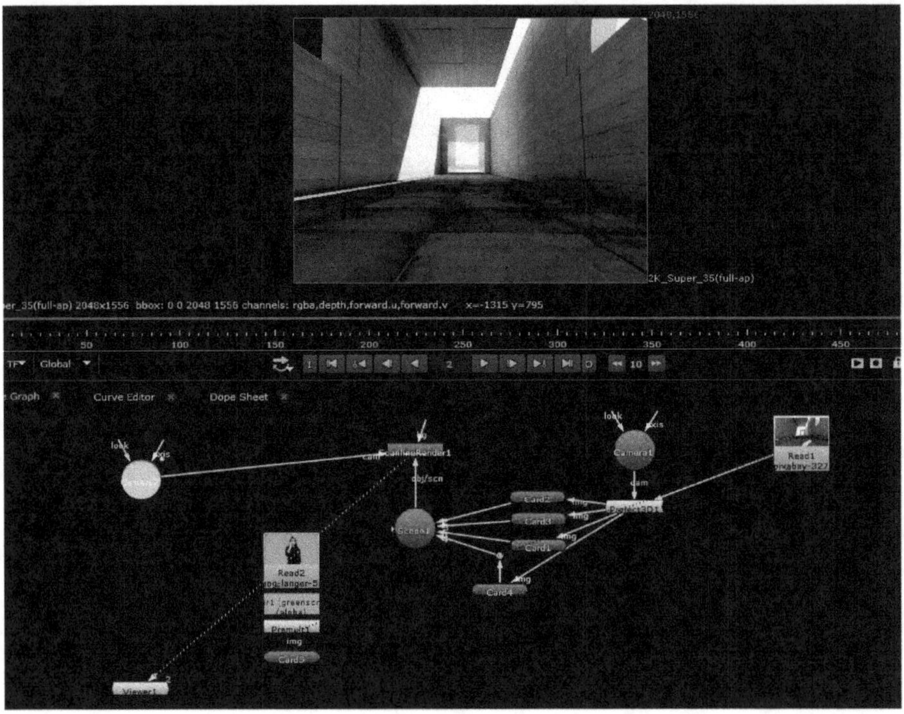

Now we have the camera Projected set , we have a virtual camera in 3D software, now what we can do is we can shoot the subject in front of a green screen and then we can remove the green background and place it in front of the projected castle. This is the amazing world of VFX where you can do anything, if you know how to do it.

Matte Painting :

We have talked a lot about replacing the green screen with another background inorder to match the theme of the story or create a fake set. But how are those backgrounds made?

These backgrounds in most cases are Matte Paintings.

Understand this by an example. Suppose you want a castle in your background, So you create a castle image using photoshop with its gate, tomb,walls, road, etc. on different layers and then in compositing software you arrange them according to distance from the subject. See the following image.

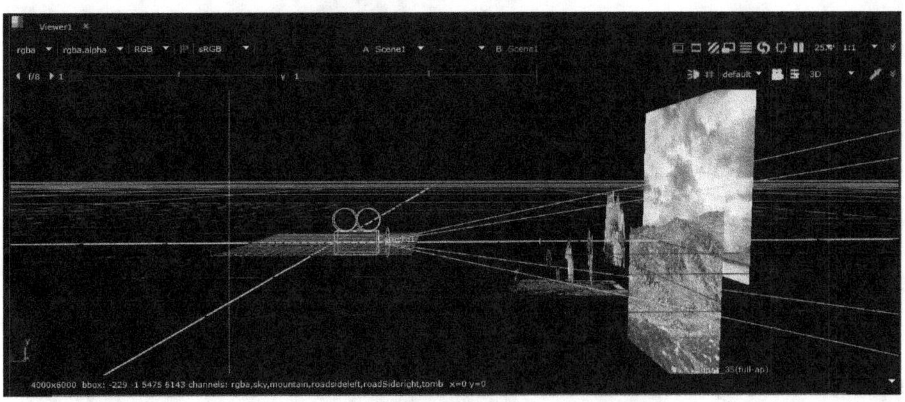

Matte Painting created having various layers so that you get the depth effect when the virtual camera moves.

This is the final output of matte paing with different layers at different distances.

This add depth to your background making it look like it's real. If you only place a photo behind your subject with no depth then it will appear fake as the virtual camera moves in your software while taking shot of different angles you want.

Sky Replacements :

In order to achieve a certain look in your shot you have to have a particular type of sky. You want a sunset scene and you have shot your video in the morning then you can replace the sky with a sunset sky and then color grade the video to make it look like a sunset shot. See the image below.

This process is similar to the process of removing the green screen. You have a blue sky in most cases which is to be replaced. Then you select the chroma color to be blue and then all your blue pixels vanish. But what if you have other blue pictures in your video. This will create problems for you. Inorder to solve this problem you have a mask option i.e you can select a region where you have to apply the chromo key.

Hence we select the sky . Now as all the pixels of sky are gone, i.e they are transparent we can now place another sky below the video so that we have a new sky. But this sky will not be attached to the background if the background is moving and all the illusion will go flop.

To make the sky stick to foreground and follow its movements we first have to track the motion of foreground using 2D Tracking which we have discussed earlier and then apply this tracking data to the sky background . And yes now our sky is replaced.

Rope Removals :

You have seen characters jumping from one building to another , or falling from a building. Or some action scene where they have a high jump , or characters may be flying. You know that these are carried out by attaching ropes to the character. But this ropes are never visible to us in final composition. How they are removed then . So let's look at how the ropes are removed using VFX. Is that a VFX ? ofcourse it is, if not then how ropes got vanished. right. First look at the manual method to understand the technique. So we have a rope in our video. A video is made up of lots of images. Let's pick the first image. Now we have to remove rope from this image. So what you use a clone tool and paint the areas of rope with the tool. Now what is a clone tool. What clone tool does is that it pick up a part of image and as you paint it on other area , the selected part get's painted over it. So using a clone tool you fill the pixels of rope with other similiar pixels. So in manual work we paint it over each frame of the video and the wire is vanished. But how to do it fastand automatically. So this canbe done using compositing software where you can define the rope using a vector line that this is the rope and then animate the line accorrding to motion of rope because the rope is not going to be at one position throught the video. Then the software automatically calculates and fill the rope pixels with its adjacent pixels.And your rope is removed.

VIII
Case Studies

Now we will Understand how all the concepts discussed in the book earlier are applied by looking at few examples.

Harry Potter

This movie doesn't need any introduction . Let's go through the following images and understand how they were changed to what they are using VFX.

You can see two images , the first one is shot on the set and another is the final shot of the movie. Now let's understand how they actually made it. You will see that in the first shot we have a blue screen .As we discussed before it is used to remove background.Also you will see some markers on the blue screen. So first matchmoving will be done because it's not a still frame , the video has a motion, so in order to match the background with foreground motion , in order that it remains still you first have to track the markers.Then you have to remove blue green and then place your background image behind the foreground layer, so it appears that it's the background of the scene. The background of the scene is Matte Painting which we have discussed in the Compositing part. And yes your shot is ready in terms of VFX.

In this image you will see that the flame of fire is added using VFX. This fire is designed by the FX department using the 3D software by creating fire simulations and then they are placed into the desired position. But this is not as simple as it sounds. What if the shot is not flat but it has a perspective. Let's say in the above shot the camera is moving 360 around the base of fire. So the fire must also have a 360 look . So that's why the shot is first 3D tracked and then a virtual camera is created in 3D software and now the camera has the same movement as that of the shot.So now this camera is used to shoot the fire and hence we have the fire with the same camera movements which can now be placed at desired place. Also note that here we not only have to track the camera but also track the object where we have to place the fire so that in the 3d software we have a reference object and can link the fire to that object so that it stays attached to the object.

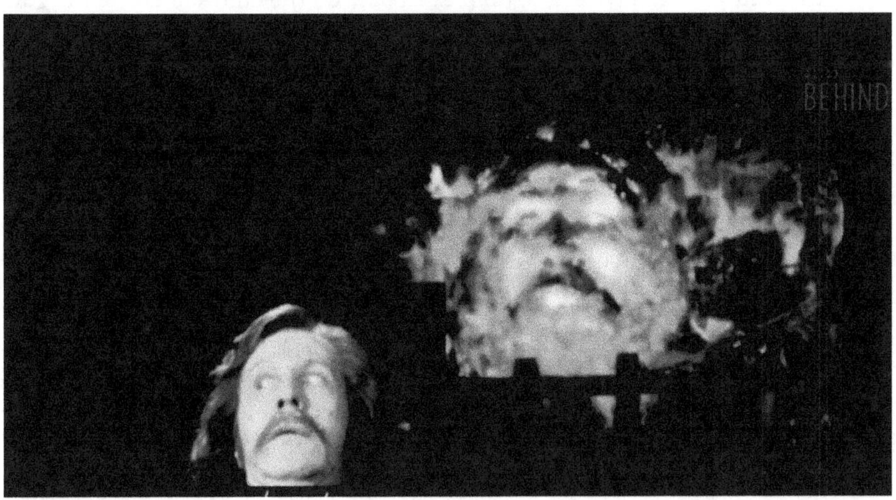

In this shot you have a man on fire and he is speaking and having some facial expressions.The man in fire you see is created using the technique of 3Dmodelling and sculpting. You can see some dots on the face of the man in the shot.These dots are used as tracking markers to track the facial expression . And then this data is put onto the 3D modelled face so that it follows the same motion as that of face. This technique is called Motion Capture.

In this Image you have a dragon placed behind the character. The dragon is a computer generated by 3D modelling . Then using FX , the fire and smoke are added to the dragon. And then placed behind the character in the shot . But wait, how they placed it behind the character. First the very important task was Matchmoving in order to place the 3 D character in frame. Once it is placed, it will overlap over the character and not go behind it. In order to do so we take the shot and roto the character , i.e we cut the character and then place it on top of the frame which has cg dragon. So it appears that the dragon is behind the character.

GAME OF THRONES:

Game of Thrones is one of the most popular web series of all time. It has a very great work of Visual Effects. You must see this piece of Art. I have not seen this web series,as I only see the VFX breakdowns. But this is one of the great web series in terms of Visual Effects.

The above images show some props with Tracking Markers. These props will be later replaced by Computer Generated dragons. As we discussed cgi. Here they create the dragons using sculpting and 3D modelling , they texture it, animate it . Then the above shot comes into play and hence the first thing that is done is Matchmoving as always. Here Camera is tracked as well as Object Trackingis also done. That is why ,as we have to track the object so the props are used in the shot so that after tracking these props , these props may be cleared and then CGI Dragons can be added to the shot. In order to remove the prop chroma keying is used with Rotoscope and paint process.

In this shot we can see a simple green screen replacement. You can clearly see the tracking markers. First these tracking markers are tracked (2D Tracking). Then they are used to solve cameras. Then the green screen is removed. But the tracking markers are not green so they don't get removed. So we have to remove them manually before the green screen is removed and after the shot is tracked. This is done by copying the color value and painting the same colour onto the markers and when the chroma key is done all the background is removed. Now then we place a Matte painting beneath the shot.

www.ingramcontent.com/pod-product-compliance
Lightning Source LLC
Chambersburg PA
CBHW050620160726
48003CB00003B/1260